Born in 1990

By

Kerry Butters.

In the Year 1990.

Millennium:	**2nd millennium**
Centuries:	19th century – **20th century** – 21st century
Decades:	1960s 1970s 1980s – **1990s** – 2000s 2010s 2020s
Years:	1987 1988 1989 – **1990** – 1991 1992 1993

1990 (MCMXC) was a common year starting on Monday (dominical letter G) of the Gregorian calendar, the 1990th year of the Common Era (CE) and *Anno Domini* (AD) designations, the 990th year of the 2nd millennium, the 90th year of the 20th century, and the 1st year of the 1990s decade.

Important events of **1990** include the Reunification of Germany and Yemeni unification, the formal beginning of the Human Genome Project (finished in 2003), the launch of the Hubble Space Telescope, the separation of Namibia from South Africa, and the Baltic states declaring independence from the Soviet Union amidst Perestroika. Yugoslavia's communist regime collapses amidst increasing internal tensions and multiparty elections held within its constituent republics result in separatist governments being elected in most of the republics marking the beginning of the breakup of Yugoslavia. Also in this year began the crisis that would lead to the Gulf War in 1991 following the Iraqi invasion and the largely internationally unrecognized annexation of Kuwait resulting in a crisis in the Persian Gulf involving the issue of the sovereignty of Kuwait and fears by Saudi Arabia over Iraqi aggression against their oil fields near Kuwait, this resulted in Operation Desert Shield being enacted with an international coalition of military forces being built up on the Kuwaiti-Saudi border with demands for Iraq to peacefully withdraw from Kuwait. Also in this year, Nelson Mandela was released from prison, and Margaret Thatcher resigned as Prime Minister of the United Kingdom after over 11 years.

1990 was an important year in the Internet's early history. In the fall of 1990, Tim Berners-Lee created the first web server and the foundation for the World Wide Web. Test operations began around December 20 and it was released outside of CERN the following year. 1990 also saw the official decommissioning of the ARPANET, a forerunner of the Internet system and the introduction of the first content search engine, Archie on September 10.

September 14, 1990 saw the first case of successful somatic gene therapy on a patient.

Due to the early 1990s recession that began that year and uncertainty due to the collapse of the socialist governments in Eastern Europe, birth rates in many countries stopped rising or fell steeply in 1990. In most western countries the Echo Boom peaked in 1990; fertility rates declined thereafter.

Encyclopædia Britannica, which ceased printing in 2012, saw its highest all time sales in 1990; 120,000 volumes were sold that year. The number of librarians in the United States also peaked around 1990.

Contents

Events

January

January 7: The Pisa tower closed.

- January 1
  - Poland becomes the first country in Eastern Europe to begin abolishing its state socialist economy. Poland also withdraws from the Warsaw Pact.
  - Glasgow begins its year as European Capital of Culture.
  - Rowan Atkinson's *Mr. Bean* debuts in a Thames Television special.
- January 3 – United States invasion of Panama: General Manuel Noriega, the deposed "strongman of Panama", surrenders to American forces.

- January 4 – Two trains collide in Sangi, Pakistan, killing between 200 and 300 people and injuring an estimated 700 others.
- January 7 – The Leaning Tower of Pisa is closed to the public because of safety concerns.
- January 9 – Ugandan Lt. Gen. Bazilio Olara-Okello, who led a coup against Dr. Apolo Milton Obote's government, dies in Ormduruman Hospital in Khartoum, Sudan.
- January 11 – Cold War: In Lithuania, 300,000 demonstrate for independence.
- January 15
  - The National Assembly of Bulgaria votes to end one party rule by the Bulgarian Communist Party.
  - Thousands storm the Stasi headquarters in East Berlin in an attempt to view their government records.
  - Martin Luther King Day Crash – Telephone service in Atlanta, St. Louis, and Detroit, including 9-1-1 service, goes down for nine hours, due to an AT&T software bug.
- January 17 – Smith & Wesson introduce the .40 S&W cartridge.
- January 20
  - Cold War: Soviet troops occupy Baku, Azerbaijan, under the state of emergency decree issued by Soviet premier Mikhail Gorbachev, and kill over 130 and wound over 700 protesters for national independence.
  - Clashes break out between Indian troops and Muslim separatists in Kashmir.
  - The government of Haiti declares a state of siege, under which it suspends civil liberties, imposes censorship,

and arrests political opponents. The state of siege is lifted on January 29.

- January 22
  - The League of Communists of Yugoslavia votes to give up its monopoly on power.
  - Robert Tappan Morris is convicted of releasing the Morris worm.
- January 25
  - Avianca Flight 52 crashes into Cove Neck, Long Island, New York after a miscommunication between the flight crew and JFK Airport officials, killing 73 people on board.
  - Prime Minister of Pakistan Benazir Bhutto gives birth to a girl, becoming the first modern head of government to bear a child while in office.
  - Pope John Paul II begins an eight-day tour of Cape Verde, Guinea-Bissau, Mali, Burkina Faso, and Chad.
- January 25–26 – The Burns' Day storm kills 97 in northwestern Europe.
- January 27 – The city of Tiraspol in the Moldavian SSR briefly declares independence.
- January 28 – Four months after their exit from power, the Polish United Workers' Party votes to dissolve itself and reorganize itself as the Social Democracy of the Republic of Poland.
- January 29
  - The trial of Joseph Hazelwood, former skipper of the *Exxon Valdez*, begins in Anchorage, Alaska. He is accused of negligence that resulted in America's second worst oil spill to date.

- In Holmdel, New Jersey, scientists at Bell Labs announce they have created a digital optical processor that could lead to the development of superfast computers that use pulses of light rather than electric currents to make calculations.
- January 31
  - Globalization – The first McDonald's in Moscow, Russia opens 8 months after construction began on 3 May 1989. 8 months later the first McDonald's in Mainland China is opened in Shenzhen.
  - Liberal Muslim Rashad Khalifa is murdered in Tucson, Arizona; his killer is theorized to be a member of an early al-Qaeda sleeper cell.
  - President of the United States George H. W. Bush gives his first State of the Union address and proposes that the U.S. and the Soviet Union make deep cuts to their military forces in Europe.

January 29: Trial relating to *Exxon Valdez*.

February

- February – Smoking is banned on all cross-country flights in the United States.
- February 2 – Apartheid in South Africa: F. W. de Klerk announces the unbanning of the African National Congress and promises to release Nelson Mandela.
- February 7

- The Communist Party of the Soviet Union votes to end its monopoly of power, clearing the way for multiparty elections.
- In the Tajik Soviet Socialist Republic, rioting breaks out against the settlement of Armenian refugees there.
- February 10
  - President of South Africa F. W. de Klerk announces that Nelson Mandela will be released the next day.
  - Las Cruces Bowling Alley massacre: 2 people walked into the 10 Pin Alley in Las Cruces, New Mexico, (known then as the Las Cruces Bowl) and shot seven people, four of whom were killed. The case is currently unsolved.
- February 11 – Nelson Mandela is released from Victor Verster Prison, near Cape Town, South Africa, after 27 years behind bars.
- February 12 – Representatives of NATO and the Warsaw Pact meet in Ottawa for an "Open Skies" conference. The conference results in agreements about superpower troop levels in Europe and on German reunification.
- February 13
  - German reunification: An agreement is reached for a two-stage plan to reunite Germany.
  - Drexel Burnham Lambert files for bankruptcy protection, Chapter 11.
- February 14 – The Pale Blue Dot photograph of Earth is sent back from the *Voyager 1* probe after completing its primary mission, from around 3.5 billion miles away.
- February 15

- The United Kingdom and Argentina restore diplomatic relations after 8 years. The UK had severed ties in response to Argentina's invasion of the Falkland Islands, a British Dependent Territory, in 1982.
- In Cartagena, Colombia, a summit is held between President of the United States George H. W. Bush, President of Bolivia Jaime Paz Zamora, President of Colombia Virgilio Barco Vargas, and President of Peru Alan García. The leaders pledge additional cooperation in fighting international drug trafficking.

- February 26
  - The Sandinistas are defeated in the Nicaraguan elections, with Violeta Chamorro elected as the new president of Nicaragua (the first elected woman president in the Americas), replacing Daniel Ortega.
  - The USSR agrees to withdraw all 73,500 troops from Czechoslovakia by July, 1991.
- February 27 – Exxon *Valdez* oil spill: Exxon and its shipping company are indicted on 5 criminal counts.
- February 28 – President of Nicaragua Daniel Ortega announces a cease-fire with the U.S.-backed *contras*.

March

- March 1
  - A fire at the Sheraton Hotel in Cairo, Egypt, kills 16 people.
  - Steve Jackson Games is raided by the U.S. Secret Service, prompting the later formation of the Electronic Frontier Foundation.

- The Royal New Zealand Navy discontinues its daily rum ration.
  - Luis Alberto Lacalle, a grandson of the late politician and diplomat Luis Alberto de Herrera, is sworn in as President of Uruguay.
- March 3 – The International Trans-Antarctic Scientific Expedition, a group of six explorers from six nations, completes the first dog sled crossing of Antarctica.
- March 6 – An SR-71 sets a U.S. transcontinental speed record of 1 hour 8 minutes 17 seconds, on what is publicized as its last official flight.
- March 8 – The Nintendo World Championships were held within the Fair Park's Automobile Building, kick starting an almost year long gaming competition across 29 American cities.
- March 9
  - Police seal off Brixton in South London after another night of protests against the poll tax.
  - Newfoundland Premier Clyde Wells confirms he will rescind Newfoundland's approval of the Meech Lake Accord.
- March 10 – Eighteen months after seizing power in a coup, Prosper Avril is ousted in Haiti.
- March 11 – Cold War: Lithuania declares independence from the Soviet Union with the Act of the Re-Establishment of the State of Lithuania.
- March 12
  - Cold War: Soviet soldiers begin leaving Hungary under terms of an agreement to withdraw all Soviet troops by June 1.

- Patricio Aylwin is sworn in as the first democratically elected Chilean president since 1970.
- March 13 – The Supreme Soviet of the Soviet Union approves changes to the Constitution of the Soviet Union to create a strong U.S.-style presidency. Mikhail Gorbachev is elected to a five-year term as the first-ever President of the Soviet Union on March 15.
- March 15
  - Iraq hangs British journalist Farzad Bazoft for spying. Daphne Parish, a British nurse, is sentenced to 15 years' imprisonment as an accomplice.
  - The first high speed (T1) transatlantic Internet connection is made over the TAT-8 fiber optic cable between CERN and Cornell University, allowing faster Internet communication between North America and Europe.
  - Mikhail Gorbachev is elected as the first executive president of the Soviet Union.
  - Cold War: The Soviet Union announces that Lithuania's declaration of independence is invalid.
  - Fernando Collor de Mello takes office as President of Brazil, Brazil's first democratically elected president since Jânio Quadros in 1961. The next day, he announces a currency freeze and freezes large bank accounts for 18 months.
- March 18
  - Twelve paintings and a Shang dynasty vase, collectively worth $100 to $300 million, are stolen from the Isabella Stewart Gardner Museum in Boston, Massachusetts by two thieves posing as police officers.

This is the largest art theft in US history, and the paintings (as of 2015) have not been recovered.

- Cold War: East Germany holds its first free elections.
- March 20 – Ferdinand Marcos's widow, Imelda Marcos, goes on trial for bribery, embezzlement, and racketeering.
- March 21 – After 75 years of South African rule since World War I, Namibia becomes independent.
- March 24 – In the Australian federal election, the Australian Labor Party, led by Prime Minister of Australia Bob Hawke, clings to power with a reduced majority.
- March 25
  - In New York City, a fire due to arson at an illegal social club called "Happy Land" kills 87.
  - Archbishop of Canterbury Robert Runcie announces his intention to retire at the end of the year.
  - In the Hungarian parliamentary election, Hungary's first multiparty election since 1948, the Hungarian Democratic Forum wins the most seats.
- March 26 – The 62nd Academy Awards, hosted by Billy Crystal, are held at the Dorothy Chandler Pavilion in Los Angeles, California, with *Driving Miss Daisy* winning Best Picture.
- March 27 – The United States begins broadcasting TV Martí to Cuba.
- March 28 – U.S. President George H. W. Bush posthumously awards Jesse Owens the Congressional Gold Medal.
- March 30 – After its first free elections on March 18, the Estonian SSR declares the Soviet rule to have been illegal since 1940 and declares a transition period for full independence.

- March 31 – "The Second Battle of Trafalgar": A massive anti-poll tax demonstration in Trafalgar Square, London, turns into a riot; 471 people are injured, and 341 are arrested.

April

- April 1
    - The Community Charge (poll tax) takes effect in England and Wales amid widespread protests
    - Strangeways Prison riot: The longest prison riot in Britain's history begins at Strangeways Prison in Manchester, and continues for 3 weeks and 3 days, until April 25.
    - The Ultimate Warrior defeats Hulk Hogan to win the WWF Championship in a Title for Title, winner takes all match at WrestleMania VI in front of nearly 68,000 people at the SkyDome in Toronto, Ontario.
    - The 1990 United States Census begins. There are 248,709,873 residents in the U.S.
- April 6 – Robert Mapplethorpe's "The Perfect Moment" show of nude and homoerotic photographs opens at the Cincinnati Contemporary Arts Center, in spite of accusations of indecency by Citizens for Community Values.
- April 7
    - Iran–Contra affair: John Poindexter is found guilty of 5 charges for his part in the scandal; the convictions are later reversed on appeal.
    - *Scandinavian Star*, a Bahamas-registered ferry, catches fire en route from Norway to Denmark, leaving 158 dead.

- April 8
  - In Nepal, Birendra of Nepal lifts a ban on political parties following violent protests.
  - In the Greek legislative election, the conservative New Democracy wins the most seats in the Hellenic Parliament; its leader, Konstantinos Mitsotakis, becomes Prime Minister of Greece on April 11.
  - In the Socialist Federal Republic of Yugoslavia, the Socialist Republic of Slovenia holds Yugoslavia's first multiparty election since 1938. After the election, a center-right coalition led by Lojze Peterle forms Yugoslavia's first non-Communist government since 1945.
- April 9 – Comet Austin, the brightest comet visible from Earth since 1975, makes its closest approach to the sun.
- April 12 – Lothar de Maizière becomes prime minister of East Germany, heading a conservative coalition that favors German reunification.
- April 13 – Cold War: The Soviet Union apologizes for the Katyn massacre.
- April 15 – Food poisoning kills 450 guests at an engagement party in Uttar Pradesh.
- April 14 – Junk bond financier Michael Milken pleaded guilty to fraud-related charges. He agreed to pay US$500 million in restitution and was sentenced on November 21 to 10 years in jail.
- April 22
  - Lebanon hostage crisis: Lebanese kidnappers release American educator Robert Polhill, who had been held hostage since January 1987.

- o Earth Day 20 is celebrated by millions worldwide.
- April 24
    - o Cold War: West Germany and East Germany agree to merge currency and economies on July 1.
    - o *STS-31*: The Hubble Space Telescope is launched aboard Space Shuttle *Discovery*.
    - o President of Zaire Mobutu Sese Seko lifts a 20-year ban on opposition parties.
- April 25 – Violeta Chamorro is elected President of Nicaragua, the first woman elected in her own right as a head of state in the Americas.
- April 28 – Liverpool F.C. win their 18th and as to date last English Football League Title when they beat Queens Park Rangers 2-1 at Anfield thanks to goals from Ian Rush and John Barnes. Their nearest challengers Aston Villa can only draw 3-3 at home to Norwich City.
- April 30 – Lebanon hostage crisis: Lebanese kidnappers release American educator Frank H. Reed, who had been held hostage since September 1986.

May

- May 1 – The former Episcopal Church in the Philippines (supervised by the Episcopal Church of the United States of America) is granted full autonomy and raised to the state of an Autocephalous Anglican province and renamed the Episcopal Church of the Philippines.
- May 2 – In London, a man brandishing a knife robs a courier of bearer bonds worth £292 million (the second largest mugging to date).

- May 2–4 – First talks between the government of South Africa and the African National Congress.
- May 4 – Latvia declares independence from the Soviet Union.
- May 6–13 – Pope John Paul II visits Mexico.
- May 8
  - Estonian SSR restores the formal name of the country, the Republic of Estonia, as well as other national emblems (the coat of arms, the flag and the anthem).
  - Rafael Ángel Calderón Fournier assumes office as President of Costa Rica.
- May 9 – In South Korea, police battle anti-government protesters in Seoul and two other cities.
- May 13 – In the Philippines, gunmen kill two United States Air Force airmen near Clark Air Base on the eve of talks between the Philippines and the United States over the future of American military bases in the Philippines.
- May 15
  - The pro-Soviet Intermovement attempts to take power in Tallinn, Estonia, but are forced down by local Estonians.
  - *Portrait of Dr. Gachet* by Vincent van Gogh is sold for a record $82.5 million.
- May 17 – The World Health Organization removes homosexuality from its list of diseases. This marked the beginning of a slow change towards public acceptance of homosexuality which is still ongoing.
- May 18 – German reunification: East Germany and West Germany sign a treaty to emerge their economic and social systems, effective July 1.

- May 19 – The US and the USSR agree to end production of chemical weapons and to destroy most of their stockpiles of chemical weapons.
- May 20 – Cold War: The first post-Communist presidential and parliamentary elections are held in Romania.
- May 21 – In Kashmir, a Kashmiri Islamic leader is assassinated and Indian security forces open fire on mourners carrying his body, killing at least 47 people.
- May 22
    - Cold War: The leaders of the Yemen Arab Republic and the People's Democratic Republic of Yemen announce the unification of their countries as the Republic of Yemen.
    - Microsoft releases Windows 3.0.
- May 27
    - In the Burmese general election, Burma's first multiparty election in 30 years, the National League for Democracy led by Aung San Suu Kyi wins in a landslide, but the State Law and Order Restoration Council nullifies the election results.
    - In the Colombian presidential election, César Gaviria is elected President of Colombia; he takes office on August 7.
- May 29
    - Mikhail Gorbachev arrives in Ottawa for a 29-hour visit.
    - Boris Yeltsin is elected as the first ever elected president of the Russian Soviet Federative Socialist Republic.
    - European Bank for Reconstruction and Development (EBRD) founded.

- May 30 – George H. W. Bush and Mikhail Gorbachev begin a four-day summit meeting in Washington, D.C.

June

- June – Joanne Rowling gets the idea for Harry Potter while on a train from Manchester to London Euston railway station. She begins writing *Harry Potter and the Philosopher's Stone* which will be completed in 1995 and published in 1997.
- June 1
  - Cold War: U.S. President George H. W. Bush and Soviet Union leader Mikhail Gorbachev sign a treaty to end chemical weapon production and begin destroying their respective stocks.
  - Members of the Provisional Irish Republican Army shoot and kill Major Michael Dillon-Lee and Private William Robert Davies of the British Army. Dillon-Lee is killed outside his home in Dortmund, Germany and Davies is killed at a railway station in Lichfield, England.
- June 2
  - The Lower Ohio Valley tornado outbreak spawns 88 confirmed tornadoes in Illinois, Indiana, Kentucky, and Ohio, killing 12; 37 tornadoes occur in Indiana, eclipsing the previous record of 21 during the Super Outbreak of April 1974.
  - Namibia recognizes the Sahrawi Arab Democratic Republic (SADR).

- June 4 – Violence breaks out in the Kirghiz Soviet Socialist Republic between the majority Kyrgyz people and minority Uzbeks over the distribution of homestead land.
- June 7
  - Metropolitan Alexy of Leningrad is elected Russian Orthodox Patriarch of Moscow and all Rus'.
  - Nickelodeon Studios opens
  - Universal Studios Orlando opens
- June 8
  - The 1990 FIFA World Cup begins in Italy. This was the first broadcast of digital HDTV in history; Europe would not begin HDTV broadcasting en masse until 2004.
  - Prime Minister of Israel Yitzhak Shamir ends 88 days with only an acting government by forming a coalition of right-wing and religious parties led by Shamir's Likud party.
- June 8–9 – In the Czechoslovakian parliamentary election, Czechoslovakia's first free election since 1946, the Civic Forum wins the most seats but fails to secure a majority.
- June 9 – *Mega Borg* oil spill in the Gulf of Mexico near Galveston, Texas.
- June 10
  - Alberto Fujimori is elected President of Peru; he takes office on July 28.
  - First round of the Bulgarian Constitutional Assembly election sees the Bulgarian Socialist Party win a majority. The second round of voting is held June 17.
- June 12

- Cold War: The Congress of People's Deputies of the Russian Federation formally declares its sovereignty.
- In the Algerian local elections, Algeria's first multiparty election since 1962, the Islamic Salvation Front wins control of more than half of municipalities and 32 of Algeria's 48 provinces.
- June 13
  - Cold War – The destruction of the Berlin Wall by East Germany officially starts, 7 months after it was opened the previous November.
  - June 13–15 – June 1990 Mineriad: Clashes break out in Bucharest between supporters and opponents of the ruling National Salvation Front.
- June 17–30 – Nelson Mandela tours North America, visiting 3 Canadian and 8 U.S. cities.
- June 19 – The Communist Party of the Russian Soviet Federative Socialist Republic is founded in Moscow.
- June 21 – The 7.4 Mw Manjil–Rudbar earthquake affects northern Iran with a maximum Mercalli intensity of X (*Extreme*), killing 35,000–50,000, and injuring 60,000–105,000.
- June 22
  - Underwater volcano Mount Didicas erupts in the Philippines.
  - Cold War: Checkpoint Charlie is dismantled.
- June 23 – In Canada, the Meech Lake Accord of 1987 dies after the Manitoba and Newfoundland legislatures fail to approve it ahead of the deadline.
- June 24 – Kathleen Young and Irene Templeton are ordained as priests in St Anne's Cathedral in Belfast, becoming the first female Anglican priests in the United Kingdom.

July

- July 1 – German reunification: East Germany and West Germany merge their economies. The Inner German border (constructed 1945) also ceases operations after operating since World War II.
- July 2
  - A stampede in a pedestrian tunnel leading to Mecca kills 1,426.
  - A U.S. District Court acquits Imelda Marcos on racketeering and fraud charges.
- July 5 – In Kenya, riots erupt against the Kenya African National Union's monopoly on power.
- July 6
  - President of Bulgaria Petar Mladenov resigns over charges he order tanks to disperse antigovernment protests in December 1989.
  - Somali president Siad Barre's bodyguards massacre anti-government demonstrators during a soccer match; 65 people are killed, more than 300 seriously injured.
- July 7–8 – Martina Navratilova of the United States wins the 1990 Wimbledon Championships – Women's Singles and Stefan Edberg of Sweden wins the 1990 Wimbledon Championships – Men's Singles.
- July 8 – West Germany defeats Argentina 1–0 to win the 1990 FIFA World Cup.
- July 9–11 – The 16th G7 summit is held in Houston.
- July 11 – Terrorists blow up passenger bus moving from Kelbecer to Tartar. 14 people were killed, 35 were wounded.

- July 15 – Tamil Tigers kill 168 Muslims in Colombo, Sri Lanka.
- July 16 – An earthquake measuring 7.7 on the Richter magnitude scale kills more than 1,600 in the Philippines.
- July 22 – First round of the Mongolian legislative election, the first multiparty ever held in Mongolia; the Mongolian People's Party wins by a wide margin after the second round of voting on July 29.
- July 25
    - George Carey, Bishop of Bath and Wells, is named as the new Archbishop of Canterbury.
    - The Serbian Democratic Party declares the sovereignty of the Serbs in Croatia.
- July 26 – U.S. President George H. W. Bush signs the Americans with Disabilities Act, designed to protect disabled Americans from discrimination.
- July 27
    - The parliament building and a government television house in Port of Spain, Trinidad and Tobago are stormed by the Jamaat al Muslimeen in a coup d'état attempt which lasts 5 days. Approximately 26 to 30 people are killed and several are wounded (including then Prime Minister, A. N. R. Robinson, who is shot in the leg).
    - Cold War: Belarus declares its sovereignty, a key step toward independence from the USSR.
- July 28 – Alberto Fujimori becomes president of Peru.
- July 28 – First Walmart in California and on the West Coast opens in Lancaster.

- July 30 – A Provisional Irish Republican Army car bomb kills former British politician and former Member of Parliament Ian Gow outside his home in England.

August

Gulf War Begins

- August 1
  - The National Assembly of Bulgaria elects Zhelyu Zhelev as the first non-Communist President of Bulgaria in 40 years.
  - RELCOM is created in the Soviet Union by combining several computer networks. Later in August, the Soviet Union got its first connection to the Internet.
- August 2
  - Gulf War: Iraq invades Kuwait, eventually leading to the Gulf War.
  - The first ban of smoking in bars in the US (and possibly the world) is passed in San Luis Obispo, California.
- August 6
  - Gulf War: The United Nations Security Council orders a global trade embargo against Iraq in response to its invasion of Kuwait.

- President of Pakistan Ghulam Ishaq Khan dismisses Prime Minister of Pakistan Benazir Bhutto, accusing her of corruption and abuse of power.
- The South African government and ANC begin talks on ending Apartheid in South Africa.
- August 7
  - U.S. President Bush orders U.S. combat planes and troops to Saudi Arabia to prevent a possible attack by Iraq.
  - Prime Minister of India V. P. Singh announces plan to reserve 49% of civil service jobs for lower-caste Hindus. The plan triggers riots, leaving at least 70 dead by September.
- August 8
  - Iraq announces that it has formally annexed Kuwait.
  - The government of Peru announces an austerity plan that results in huge increases in the price of food and gasoline. The plan sets off days of rioting and a national strike on August 21.
- August 10
  - Egypt, Syria, and 10 other Arab nations vote to send military forces to Saudi Arabia to discourage an invasion from Iraq.
  - A passenger bus, traveling along the route "Tbilisi-Agdam", is blown up; 20 people died and 30 were injured. Organizers of the crime, Armenians A. Avanesian and M. Tatevosian, were brought to criminal trial.
- August 12

- In South Africa, fighting breaks out between the Xhosa people and the Zulu people; more than 500 people are killed by the end of August.
- "Sue", the best preserved *Tyrannosaurus rex* specimen ever found, is discovered near Faith, South Dakota by Sue Hendrickson.
- August 19 – Leonard Bernstein conducts his final concert, ending with Ludwig van Beethoven's Symphony No. 7 performed by the Boston Symphony Orchestra.
- August 21 – Gambia, Ghana, Guinea, Nigeria, and Sierra Leone send peacekeepers to intervene in the First Liberian Civil War.
- August 22 – U.S. President Bush calls up U.S. military reservists for service in the Persian Gulf Crisis.
- August 23 – East Germany and West Germany announce they will unite on October 3.
- August 24
  - Armenia declares its independence from the Soviet Union.
  - Northern Ireland writer Brian Keenan is released from Lebanon after being held hostage for nearly 5 years.
- August 26 – In Sofia, protesters set fire to the headquarters of the governing Bulgarian Socialist Party.
- August 28 – The Plainfield Tornado (F5 on the Fujita scale) strikes the towns of Plainfield, Crest Hill, and Joliet, Illinois, killing 29 people (the strongest tornado to date to strike the Chicago metropolitan area).

September

- September 1–10 – Pope John Paul II visits Tanzania, Burundi, Rwanda and Ivory Coast.
- September 2 – Cold War: Transnistria declares its independence from the Moldavian SSR; however, the declaration is not recognized by any government.
- September 4 – Geoffrey Palmer resigns as Prime Minister of New Zealand and is replaced by Mike Moore.
- September 4–6 – Premier of North Korea Yon Hyong-muk meets with President of South Korea Roh Tae-woo, the highest level contact between leaders of the two Koreas since 1945.
- September 5 – Sri Lankan Civil War: Sri Lankan Army soldiers kill 158 civilians.
- September 6 – In Burma, the State Law and Order Restoration Council orders the arrest of Aung San Suu Kyi and five other political dissidents.
- September 9
    - U.S. President Bush and Soviet President Gorbachev meet in Helsinki to discuss the Persian Gulf crisis.
    - First Liberian Civil War: Liberian president Samuel Doe is captured by rebel leader Prince Johnson and killed in a filmed execution.
    - Sri Lankan Civil War: Sri Lankan Army soldiers kill 184 civilians in Batticaloa.
- September 10 – First Pizza Hut opens in Soviet Union.
- September 11

- Gulf War: U.S. President George H. W. Bush delivers a nationally televised speech in which he threatens the use of force to remove Iraqi soldiers from Kuwait.
- First Pizza Hut opens in the People's Republic of China, nearly 3 years after the first KFC opened there in 1987.
- September 12
  - Cold War: The two German states and the Four Powers sign the Treaty on the Final Settlement with Respect to Germany in Moscow, paving the way for German reunification.
  - A judge in Australia orders the arrest of media tycoon Christopher Skase, former owner of the Seven Network, after he fails to give evidence in a liquidator's examination of failed shipbuilding company Lloyds Ships Holdings, an associate of Skase's Qintex Australia Ltd.
- September 17 – In what is now regarded as a landmark event in regards to women in journalism, reporter Lisa Olson was sexually harassed by multiple New England Patriots players while trying to conduct a locker room interview.
- September 18
  - The International Olympic Committee awards the 1996 Summer Olympics to Atlanta.
  - The Provisional Irish Republican Army tries to assassinate Air Chief Marshal Sir Peter Terry at his home near Stafford, England. Hit by at least 9 bullets, the former Governor of Gibraltar survives.

- September 24 – The Supreme Soviet of the Soviet Union grants Gorbachev special powers for 18 months to secure the Soviet Union's transition to a market economy.
- September 27 – David Souter is confirmed to serve on the Supreme Court, replacing retiring Justice William Brennan.
- September 29 – Washington, D.C.'s National Cathedral is finished.
- September 29–30 – The United Nations World Summit for Children draws more than 70 world leaders to United Nations Headquarters.

October

October 3: The former flag of West Germany becomes the flag of all Germany.

- October – Tim Berners-Lee begins his work on the World Wide Web, 19 months after his seminal 1989 outline of what would become the Web concept.
- October 1 – The rebel Rwandan Patriotic Front invades Rwanda from Uganda, marking the start of the Rwandan Civil War.
- October 1 – First Walmart in the Northeastern United States opens in York, Pennsylvania.
- October 3 – Cold War: East Germany and West Germany reunify into a single Germany.

- October 4 – In the Philippines, rebel forces seize two military posts on the island of Mindanao, before surrendering on October 6.
- October 8
  - Israeli–Palestinian conflict: In Jerusalem, Israeli police kill 17 Palestinians and wound over 100 near the Dome of the Rock mosque on the Temple Mount.
  - Globalization: First McDonald's restaurant is opened in Mainland China in Shenzhen, near Hong Kong. Since 1979, Shenzhen has been a Special economic zone.
- October 13 – Lebanese Civil War: Syrian military forces invade and occupy Mount Lebanon, ousting General Michel Aoun's government. This effectively consolidates Syria's 14 year occupation of Lebanese soil.
- October 14 – Composer and conductor Leonard Bernstein dies of a heart attack at his home in New York City at the age of 72.
- October 15
  - Cold War: Soviet Union leader Mikhail Gorbachev is awarded the Nobel Peace Prize for his efforts to lessen Cold War tensions and reform his nation.
  - South Africa ends segregation of libraries, trains, buses, toilets, swimming pools, and other public facilities.
- October 17 – A peace agreement which formally ended 28 years of Sarawak Communist insurgency in Malaysia was signed by North Kalimantan Communist Party insurgents
- October 24 – In the Pakistani general election, Prime Minister Bhutto's Pakistan Peoples Party loses power to a center-right coalition government.
- October 25–28 – Taxi blockade in Hungary.

- October 27 – Cold War: The Supreme Soviet of Kyrgyzstan chooses Askar Akayev as the republic's first president.
  - The New Zealand general election is won by the New Zealand National Party, and its leader, Jim Bolger, becomes prime minister.
- October 29 – In Norway, the government headed by Prime Minister of Norway Jan P. Syse collapses.
- October 30 The first transatlantic fiber optic cable TAT-8 fails, causing a slowdown of Internet traffic between the United States and Europe.

November

Margaret Thatcher, the UK's only female Prime Minister, resigns after 11 years.

- November – The earliest known portable digital camera sold in the United States ships.
- November 1 – Mary Robinson defeats odds-on favorite Brian Lenihan to become the first female President of Ireland.
- November 2 – British Satellite Broadcasting and Sky Television plc merge to form BSkyB as a result of massive losses.
- November 3 – Gro Harlem Brundtland assumes office as Prime Minister of Norway.

- November 5 – Rabbi Meir Kahane, founder of the far-right Kach movement, is shot dead after a speech at a New York City hotel.
- November 6 – Nawaz Sharif is sworn in as Prime Minister of Pakistan.
- November 7
  - Indian Prime Minister Singh resigns over losing a confidence vote in the Parliament of India, having lost the support of Hindus who want a Muslim mosque in Ayodhya torn down to build a Hindu temple.
  - Final military parade to mark the anniversary of the October Socialist Revolution takes place in the Soviet Union.
- November 9
  - A new constitution comes into effect in the Kingdom of Nepal, establishing multiparty democracy and constitutional monarchy; this is the culmination of the 1990 People's Movement.
  - The Parliament of Singapore enacts the Maintenance of Religious Harmony Act.
- November 10 – Chandra Shekhar becomes Prime Minister of India as head of a minority government.
- November 12
  - Akihito is enthroned as the 125th emperor of Japan following the death of his father on January 7, 1989.
  - Tim Berners-Lee publishes a more formal proposal for the World Wide Web.
- November 13
  - The first known web page is written.

- In New Zealand, David Gray kills 13 people in what will become known as the Aramoana massacre.
- November 14 – Germany and Poland sign a treaty confirming the border at the Oder–Neisse line.
- November 15 – *STS-38*: Space Shuttle *Atlantis* is launched on a classified U.S. military mission.
  - President Bush signed new Clean Air Act, focused on urban pollution and cancer-causing emissions from industrial sources.
- November 16 – *Home Alone* is released to theaters. It would become the highest grossing live-action family comedy film of all time.
- November 17 – Soviet President Gorbachev proposes a radical restructuring of the Soviet government, including the creation of a Federal Council to be made up of the heads of the 15 Soviet republics.
- November 19-21 – Leaders of Canada, the United States, and 32 European nations meet in Paris to formally mark the end of the Cold War.
- November 21
  - Charter of Paris for a New Europe signed.
  - Agreement for decriminalization of homosexual acts between consenting adults in Queensland.
  - The second Nintendo video game console Super Famicom is released in Japan.
- November 22 – Margaret Thatcher announces she will not contest the second ballot of the leadership election for the Conservative Party (UK).
- November 25 – Lech Wałęsa and Stanisław Tymiński win the first round of the first Polish presidential election.

- November 27 – Women's suffrage is introduced in the last Swiss half-canton of Appenzell Innerrhoden.
- November 28
  - Prime Minister of Singapore Lee Kuan Yew resigns and is replaced by Goh Chok Tong.
  - Prime Minister of the United Kingdom Margaret Thatcher resigns and is replaced by John Major.
- November 29
  - Gulf War: The United Nations Security Council passes UN Security Council Resolution 678, authorizing military intervention in Iraq if that nation does not withdraw its forces from Kuwait and free all foreign hostages by Tuesday, January 15, 1991.
  - Prime Minister of Bulgaria Andrey Lukanov and his government of former Communists resign under pressure from strikes and street protests.

December

- December 1
  - Channel Tunnel workers from the United Kingdom and France meet 40 metres beneath the English Channel seabed, establishing the first land connection between Great Britain and the mainland of Europe for around 8,000 years.
  - President of Chad Hissène Habré is deposed by the Patriotic Salvation Movement and replaced as president by its leader Idriss Déby.

- December 2 – The German federal election (the first election held since German reunification) is won by Helmut Kohl, who becomes Chancellor of Germany.
- December 3
  - At Detroit Metropolitan Airport, Northwest Airlines Flight 1482 (a McDonnell Douglas DC-9) collides with Northwest Airlines Flight 299 (a Boeing 727) on the runway, killing 8 passengers and 4 crew members on Flight 1482.
  - Mary Robinson begins her term as President of Ireland, becoming the first female to hold this office.
- December 6
  - Saddam Hussein releases the Western hostages.
  - President Hussain Muhammad Ershad of Bangladesh is forced to resign following massive protests; he is replaced by Shahabuddin Ahmed, who becomes interim president.
- December 7
  - In Brussels, trade talks break fail because of a dispute between the U.S. and the European Union over farm export subsidies.
  - The National Assembly of Bulgaria elects Dimitar Iliev Popov as Prime Minister of Bulgaria.
- December 9
  - Slobodan Milošević becomes President of Serbia.
  - Lech Wałęsa wins the 2nd round of Poland's first presidential election.
- December 16 – Jean-Bertrand Aristide is elected president of Haiti, ending 3 decades of military rule.

- December 20 – Eduard Shevardnadze announces his resignation as Soviet Minister of Foreign Affairs
  - Tim Berners-Lee completes the test for the first webpage at CERN.
- December 22
  - The first constitution of the Republic of Croatia is adopted.
  - The Marshall Islands and Federated States of Micronesia become independent, after the termination of their trusteeship.
  - The Polish government-in-exile is dissolved in London after being in exile since 1939.
- December 23 – In the Slovenian independence referendum, 88.5% of the overall electorate (94.8% of votes), with the turnout of 93.3%, supported independence of the country.
- December 24 – Ramsewak Shankar is ousted as President of Suriname by a military coup.
- December 31 – Russian Garry Kasparov holds his title by winning the World Chess Championship match against his countryman Anatoly Karpov.

Date unknown

- Satoshi Tajiri begins creating the first Pokémon game.

Births

January

Toni Kroos

Liam Hemsworth

Jake Thomas

- January 1
  - Nadia Pariss, African American pornographic actress (pt)
- January 4
  - Toni Kroos, German footballer
  - Alberto Paloschi, Italian footballer
- January 5 – Yoseob, Korean pop singer (B2ST)
- January 6
  - Abhinav Mukund, Indian cricketer
  - Dominique Aegerter, Swiss motorcycle racer
  - Alex Teixeira, Brazilian footballer
- January 7
  - Gregor Schlierenzauer, Austrian ski jumper
  - Camryn Grimes, American actress
  - Liam Aiken, American actor
  - Elene Gedevanishvili, Georgian figure skater
- January 9
  - Melissa Ricks, Filipino-American actress
  - Oteng Oteng, Batswana boxer
  - Justin Blackmon, American football player
- January 10
  - Tao Li, Singaporean Olympic swimmer
  - Jessica Scheel, Miss Guatemala Universe 2010
- January 12 – Sergey Karjakin, Ukrainian chess player
- January 13 – Liam Hemsworth, Australian actor
- January 14 – Áron Szilágyi, Hungarian fencer
- January 15
  - Fernando Forestieri, Italian footballer
  - Luke Willson, American football player
- January 17 – Tom Bosworth, British race walker

- January 22 – Alizé Cornet, French tennis player
- January 23 – Artsem Mikhalenka, Belarusian singer (3+2)
- January 24 – Mao Abe, Japanese singer-songwriter
- January 26
  - Christopher Massey, American actor
  - Kherington Payne, American dancer and actress
- January 28 – Luce, French actress/singer
- January 30
  - Eiza González, Mexican actress/singer
  - Jake Thomas, American actor and singer
- January 31 – Kota Yabu, Japanese singer/actor

February

Sean Kingston

The Weeknd

Park Shin-hye

Bea Rose Santiago

Megan Young

- February 1 – Hersi Matmuja, Albanian singer
- February 3 – Sean Kingston, American singer
- February 4 – Haruka Tomatsu, Japanese voice actress
- February 6 – Jermaine Kearse, American football player
- February 7
  - Anna Abreu, Finnish pop singer
  - Steven Stamkos, Canadian ice hockey player
- February 8 – Klay Thompson, American basketball player
- February 9 – Facundo Affranchino, Argentine footballer
- February 10 – Sooyoung, a member of South Korean girl group Girls' Generation
- February 11 – Q'orianka Kilcher, German-born actress
- February 12 – Robert Griffin III, American football player
- February 13 – Gyaincain Norbu, 11th Panchen Lama of Tibetan Buddhism according to some sources
- February 15 – Masashi Ebinuma, Japanese judoka
- February 16 – The Weeknd, Canadian musician
- February 17 – Bea Rose Santiago, Filipino model and Miss International 2013 titleholder
- February 18 – Park Shin-hye, South Korean actress
- February 19 – Luke Pasqualino, English actor
- February 21
  - David Addy, Ghanaian footballer
  - Thabiso Baholo, Lesotho swimmer
  - Mattias Tedenby, Swedish ice hockey player
- February 23
  - Kevin Cheung, Mauritian swimmer
  - Terry Hawkridge, English footballer
  - February 27
  - Lindsey Morgan, American actress

- o Megan Young, U.S.-born Filipina actress, Miss World 2013
- February 28 – Anna Muzychuk, Ukrainian chess player

March

Cassie Scerbo

- March 1 – James Lomas, British actor
- March 2 – Adderly Fong, Hong Kong Chinese race car driver
- March 3 – Celina Ree, Danish singer
- March 4 – Andrea Bowen, American actress
- March 6 – Esti Ginzburg, Israeli model
- March 7 – Abigail and Brittany Hensel, American conjoined twins
- March 8
  - o Kristinia DeBarge, American singer-songwriter
  - o Petra Kvitová, Czech tennis player
- March 14 – Joe Allen, Welsh footballer
- March 19
  - o Anthony Skorich, Australian soccer player
  - o Maddy Hill, English actress
- March 20 – Marcos Rojo, Argentine footballer

- March 21
  - Alyssa Campanella, Miss USA 2011
  - Mandy Capristo, German singer-songwriter, dancer and model
- March 23
  - Princess Eugenie of York, British Princess and daughter of Prince Andrew, Duke of York and Sarah, Duchess of York
  - Jaime Alguersuari, Spanish Formula One driver
- March 24
  - Keisha Castle-Hughes, Australian-born New Zealand actress
  - Aljur Abrenica, Filipino actor
  - Starlin Castro, Major League Baseball player
- March 25 – Kiowa Gordon, American actor
- March 26
  - Yuya Takaki, Japanese singer/actor
  - Carly Chaikin, American actress
  - Xiumin, South Korean singer (EXO)
  - James Buescher, American stock car driver
  - Patrick Ekeng, Cameroonian footballer (d. 2016)
- March 28 – Zoe Sugg, British vlogger
- March 30
  - Thomas Rhett, American singer and songwriter
  - Cassie Scerbo, American actress
- March 31 – Bang Yong-guk, South Korean rapper

April

Kristen Stewart

Emma Watson

Machine Gun Kelly

Dev Patel

- April 2
  - Miralem Pjanić, Bosnian footballer
  - Yevgeniya Kanayeva, Russian rhythmic gymnast, 3 times world champion and first and only back to back olympic champion
- April 5 – Haruma Miura, Japanese actor and singer
- April 6 –Tony Piazza, Boss
- April 8 – Kim Jonghyun, Singer from Korean group SHINee
- April 9 – Kristen Stewart, American actress
- April 10
  - Alex Pettyfer, English actor
  - Ben Amos, English footballer
- April 15 – Emma Watson, English actress
- April 16
  - Lorraine Nicholson, American actress
  - Lily Loveless, British actress
- April 17 – Astrit Ajdarević, Swedish professional football player
- April 18
  - Britt Robertson, American actress
  - Wojciech Szczęsny, Polish football player
- April 19

- o Kim Chiu, Filipino actress
- o Kim Himchan, South Korean singer
- April 20 – Lu Han, South Korean singer (EXO)
- April 22 – Machine Gun Kelly, American rapper
- April 23 – Dev Patel, British actor
- April 27 – Austin Dillon, American stock car driver
- April 30 – Madison Riley, American actress

May

Kay Panabaker

Nadine Beiler

Chris Colfer

- May 1 – Caitlin Stasey, Australian actress
- May 2 – Kay Panabaker, American actress
- May 3 – Miranda Chartrand, Canadian singer
- May 4
  - Nic Naitanui, Australian rules footballer
  - David Hasler, Liechtenstein footballer
- May 5
  - Hannah Davis, American model
  - Nicklas Pedersen, Mister World 2014 winner
  - Saad Al Sheebi, Qatari footballer
- May 8
  - Anastasia Zuyeva, Russian swimmer
  - Kemba Walker, American basketball player
- May 10
  - Karmen Pedaru, Estonian model
  - Brandun DeShay, American rapper and record producer
- May 12 – Florent Amodio, French figure skater
- May 15
  - Denzel Whitaker, American actor
- May 16
  - Thomas Brodie-Sangster, British actor

- Darko Šarović, Serbian sprinter
- May 17
  - Kree Harrison, American singer
  - Leven Rambin, American actress
- May 24
  - Joey Logano, American race car driver
  - Yuya Matsushita, Japanese singer, dancer, and actor
- May 26
  - Umar Akmal, Pakistani cricketer
- May 27
  - Nadine Beiler, Austrian R&B and Pop singer,
  - Chris Colfer, American actor
- May 30
  - Matías Nocedal, Argentine basketball player
  - Dean Collins, American actor
  - Yoona, a member of Korean girl group Girls' Generation

June

Iggy Azalea

Aaron Taylor-Johnson

John Newman

- June 2
  - Kristiina Brask, Finnish pop singer
  - Brittany Curran, American actress and singer
- June 3 – Jason Akeson, Canadian professional ice hockey player
- June 6
  - Mike G, American rapper and chopped and screwed remixer
  - Ryan Higa, American YouTuber
- June 7
  - Iggy Azalea, Australian recording artist
  - Daniel Rich, Australian rules footballer

- June 10 – Niamh Perry, Irish actress and singer
- June 11 – Christophe Lemaitre, French sprinter
- June 12 – Jrue Holiday, American basketball player
- June 13 – Aaron Taylor-Johnson, English actor
- June 15 – Miwa, Japanese singer
- June 16 – John Newman, English singer
- June 17
    - Alan Dzagoev, Russian footballer
    - Jordan Henderson, English international footballer
    - Laura Wright, English singer
- June 18 – Sandra Izbaşa, Romanian gymnast and Olympic gold medalist
- June 19 – Jason Dy, Filipino singer
- June 21
    - Ričardas Berankis, Lithuanian tennis player
    - Håvard Nordtveit, Norwegian football player
- June 22 – Kei Inoo, Japanese singer/actor
- June 23 – Vasek Pospisil, Canadian tennis player
- June 27
    - Angelia Ong, Filipino—Chinese model and Miss Earth 2015 titleholder
    - Bobby Wagner, American football player
- June 28 – Jasmine Richards, Canadian actress
- June 29 – Sayuri Sugawara, Japanese singer

July

Margot Robbie

Sosuke Ikematsu

Wizkid

James Maslow

Indiana Evans

- July 1 – Ángelo Balanta, Colombian footballer
- July 2
    - Roman Lob, German recording artist
    - Margot Robbie, Australian actress
    - David Kross, German actor
- July 6 – Jeremy Suarez, American actor
- July 9
    - Sosuke Ikematsu, Japanese actor
    - Rafael, Brazilian footballer
    - Fabio da Silva, Brazilian footballer
- July 11
    - Caroline Wozniacki, Danish tennis player
    - Patrick Peterson, American football player

- July 15
  - Olly Alexander, English actor and singer (Years & Years)
  - Damian Lillard, American basketball player
- July 16
  - James Maslow, American actor and singer
  - Wizkid, Nigerian recording artist, songwriter and performer
- July 17 – Jonty Usborne, British radio engineer
- July 18
  - Saúl Álvarez, Mexican boxer
  - Anders Konradsen, Norwegian footballer
- July 19 – Rosie Jones, English glamour model
- July 23 – Kevin Reynolds, Canadian Figure Skater
- July 24
  - Daveigh Chase, American actress
  - Jay McGuiness, British singer, part of The Wanted
- July 27
  - Nick Hogan, American television personality
  - Indiana Evans, Australian actress
- July 28 – Soulja Boy, American rapper
- July 29
  - Anna Selezneva, Russian model
  - Munro Chambers, Canadian actor
  - Shin Se-kyung, Korean actor
  - Oleg Shatov, Russian footballer
  - Joey Essex, English TV Reality star and DJ
- July 30 – Chris Maxwell, Welsh footballer

August

Jennifer Lawrence

Bo Burnham

- August 1
  - Jean Hugues Gregoire, Mauritian swimmer
  - Elton Jantjies, South African rugby player
  - Jack O'Connell, English actor
- August 3
  - Jourdan Dunn, British model
  - James Baxter, British actor
- August 9 – Adelaide Kane, Australian actress
- August 10 – Tai Woffinden, English speedway rider
- August 12 – Mario Balotelli, Italian footballer
- August 13 – Shila Amzah, Malaysian singer-songwriter
- August 15 – Jennifer Lawrence, American actress
- August 17 – Rachel Hurd-Wood, British actress

- August 20 – Ranomi Kromowidjojo, Dutch swimmer
- August 21 – Bo Burnham, American comedian
- August 27 – Madison Welch, English glamour model
- August 28
  - Bojan Krkić, Spanish footballer
  - Katie Findlay, Canadian actress
- August 29 – Nicole Anderson, American actress
- August 30 – Lưu Thị Diễm Hương, Vietnamese beauty queen

September

Allison Scagliotti

Christian Serratos

- September 3 – Abbas Ali, Pakistani footballer
- September 4
  - Olha Kharlan, Ukrainian fencer
  - Danny Worsnop, British musician
- September 5 – Kim Yuna, South Korean figure skater
- September 6
  - John Wall, American basketball player
  - Matt McAndrew, American singer-songwriter, contestant from The Voice season 7
- September 8 – Matt Barkley, American football player
- September 9
  - Melody Klaver, Dutch actress
  - Haley Reinhart, American singer
- September 13 – Jamie Anderson, American snowboarder
- September 14 – Alex Lowes and Sam Lowes, English motorcycle racers. Twin brothers
- September 19 – Saki Fukuda, Japanese actress
- September 20
  - Phillip Phillips, American singer
  - John Tavares, Canadian ice hockey player
- September 21
  - Christian Serratos, American actress
  - Allison Scagliotti, American actress
- September 23
  - Çağatay Ulusoy, Turkish model and actor
  - Marigona Dragusha, Kosovan model, Miss Universe Kosovo 2009
  - Agustín Sierra, Argentine actor
  - Laurent Alvarez, Swiss figure skater
- September 25

- Daria Strokous, Russian model
- Mao Asada, Japanese figure skater
- September 28 – Kirsten Prout, Canadian actress
- September 29 – Doug Brochu, American actor
- September 30
  - Gracie Glam, American pornographic actress
  - Dominique Aegerter, Swiss Grand prix motorcycle racer

October

Jóhanna Guðrún Jónsdóttir (Yohanna)

- October 2 – Samantha Barks, Manx singer and actress
- October 3
  - Johan Le Bon, French cyclist
  - Rhian Ramos, Filipino actress
- October 7
  - Ayla Kell, American actress
  - Thunder, South Korean pop singer, member of MBLAQ
- October 11 – Sebastian Rode, German footballer
- October 12
  - Brock Coyle, American football player

- o Henri Lansbury, English footballer
- October 16 – Jóhanna Guðrún Jónsdóttir (Yohanna), Icelandic singer and Eurovision Song Contest 2009 runner-up
- October 18 – Carly Schroeder, American actress
- October 19 – Samantha Munro, American actress
- October 21 – Ricky Rubio, Spanish basketball player
- October 22
  - o Jonathan Lipnicki, American actor
  - o Ashley Fiolek, American champion motocross racer
- October 23 – Paradise Oskar, Finnish singer-songwriter
- October 24 – İlkay Gündoğan, German footballer
- October 25 – Austin Peralta, American jazz musician and composer (d. 2012)
- October 29 – Eric Saade, Swedish pop singer
- October 31 – Noodle, member of the Gorillaz

November

Kendall Schmidt

Sarah Hyland

Rita Ora

Magnus Carlsen

- November 2 – Kendall Schmidt, American actor and singer
- November 4 – Jean-Luc Bilodeau, Canadian actor
- November 6
  - Dorothea Barth Jörgensen, Swedish model
  - Kris, South Korean singer (EXO)
  - André Schürrle, German footballer

- November 7
  - Matt Corby, Australian singer
  - Marisa Siketa, Australian actress
- November 9
  - Hodgy Beats, American rapper and record producer
  - Christine Michael, American football player
- November 14 – Jessica Jacobs, Australian actress and singer (d. 2008)
- November 15 – Kanata Hongō, Japanese actor
- November 22 – Jang Dong-woo, South Korean singer, dancer and rapper. Member of Infinite (band)
- November 24 – Sarah Hyland, American actress
- November 26
  - Rita Ora, English singer
  - Danny Welbeck, English footballer
- November 27 – Josh James, British singer
- November 28 – Sena Acolatse, American professional ice hockey player
- November 29 – Diego González, Mexican singer, actor, and songwriter
- November 30 – Magnus Carlsen, Norwegian chess grandmaster

December

JoJo

- December 1 – Chanel Iman, American Supermodel
- December 2 – Jamille Matt, Jamaican footballer
- December 3 – Sharon Fichman, Canadian/Israeli tennis player
- December 9
  - LaFee, German singer/songwriter
  - Ashleigh Brewer, Australian actress
- December 10
  - Giulia Boverio, Italian actress
  - Shoya Tomizawa, Japanese motorcycle rider (d. 2010)
- December 12 – Seungri, South Korean singer
- December 13 – Corey Anderson, New Zealand cricketer
- December 17
  - Folashade Abugan, Nigerian sprinter
  - John Rooney, English footballer
- December 18 – Lara Scandar, Egyptian singer
- December 20 – JoJo, American singer/actress
- December 22 – Jean-Baptiste Maunier, French actor
- December 23

- Anna Maria Perez de Taglé, American actress
  - Anna Mae Routledge, Canadian actress
- December 26
  - Aaron Ramsey, Welsh footballer
  - Andy Biersack, American singer-songwriter (Black Veil Brides)
- December 27 – Milos Raonic, Canadian tennis player
- December 28 – David Archuleta, American singer
- December 30 – Joe Root, English cricketer
- December 31
  - Patrick Chan, Canadian figure skater
  - Zhao Jing, Chinese swimmer

Deaths

January

Pavel Cherenkov

Barbara Stanwyck

Prince Naruhiko Higashikuni

Roman Vishniac

Ava Gardner

- January 2
  - Alan Hale, Jr., American actor (b. 1921)

- o Evangelos Averoff, Greek politician, former Foreign Minister (b. 1910)
- January 4
  - o Sir Henry Bolte, Australian politician, former Premier of Victoria (b. 1908)
  - o Harold Eugene Edgerton, American electrical engineer (b. 1903)
  - o Alberto Lleras Camargo, Colombian politician, former President of the Republic (b. 1906)
- January 5 – Arthur Kennedy, American actor (b. 1914)
- January 6
  - o Ian Charleson, Scottish actor (b. 1949)
  - o Pavel Cherenkov, Russian physicist, Nobel Prize laureate (b. 1904)
- January 7
  - o Avraham Abba Leifer, American Hassidic dynastic rabbi (1918)
  - o Bronko Nagurski, Canadian-American football player (Chicago Bears) and member of the Pro Football Hall of Fame (b. 1908)
- January 8
  - o Terry-Thomas, English actor (b. 1911)
  - o Jaime Gil de Biedma, Spanish poet (b. 1929)
- January 9
  - o Bazilio Olara-Okello, Ugandan military officer and statesman, former head of State (b. 1929)
  - o Spud Chandler, American baseball player (b. 1907)
  - o Northern Calloway, American actor, played David on Sesame Street from 1971-1989 (b. 1948)
- January 10 – Lyle R. Wheeler, American art director (b. 1905)

- January 15 – Gordon Jackson, Scottish actor (b. 1923)
- January 17 – Charles Hernu, French politician, former minister of Defense (b. 1923)
- January 18
  - Rusty Hamer, American actor (b. 1947)
  - Melanie Appleby, British musician (b. 1966)
  - Edouard Izac, Lieutenant in the United States Navy during World War I (b. 1891)
- January 19
  - Arthur Goldberg, American Justice of the Supreme Court (b. 1908)
  - Bhagwan Shree Rajneesh, Indian mystic and spiritual teacher (b. 1931)
  - Herbert Wehner, German Social Democratic politician (b. 1906)
- January 20
  - Hayedeh, Iranian singer (b. 1942)
  - Naruhiko Higashikuni, Japanese former Prime Minister (b. 1887)
  - Barbara Stanwyck, American actress (b. 1907)
- January 22
  - Mariano Rumor, Italian politician, former Prime Minister (b. 1915)
  - Roman Vishniac, Russian-American photographer (b. 1897)
- January 23
  - Allen Collins, American musician (b. 1952)
  - José Napoleón Duarte, Salvadoran politician, former President of the Republic (b. 1925)
- January 24 – Madge Bellamy, American actress (b. 1899)

- January 25
  - Ava Gardner, American actress (b. 1922)
  - Dámaso Alonso, Spanish poet (b. 1898)
- January 26 – Lewis Mumford, American historian of science (b. 1895)
- January 27 – Helen Jerome Eddy, American actress (b. 1897)
- January 28 – Joseph Payne Brennan, American poet/author (b. 1918)
- January 29 – Elise Blumann, German born artist who achieved recognition as an Australian Expressionist painter (b. 1897)
- January 30 – John Rogers Cox, American painter (b. 1915)

February

Johnnie Ray

Sandro Pertini

- February 2
  - Joe Erskine, British boxer (b. 1934)
  - Paul Ariste, Estonian linguist (b. 1905)
  - Mel Lewis, American jazz musician (b. 1929)
- February 7
  - Alfredo M. Santos, Filipino general and World War II hero (b. 1905)
  - Jimmy Van Heusen, American composer (b. 1913)
- February 8 – Del Shannon, American musician and singer (b. 1934)
- February 10 – Bill Sherwood, American film director (b. 1952)
- February 11 – Fred Jones, English footballer (b. 1898)
- February 14
  - Jean Wallace, American actress (b. 1923)
  - José Luis Panizo, Spanish footballer (b. 1922)
- February 16
  - Keith Haring, American pop artist (b. 1958)
  - Robert Ouko, Kenyan politician (b. 1931)
- February 17
  - Erik Rhodes, American actor (b. 1906)
  - Brendan Corish, Irish labour politician (b. 1918)
- February 19
  - Otto E. Neugebauer, Austrian-American mathematician and historian of science (b. 1899)
  - Michael Powell, British director (b. 1905)
  - Edris Rice-Wray Carson, M.D., medical researcher (b. 1904)
- February 23 – James M. Gavin, American general (b. 1907)
- February 24

- o Malcolm Forbes, American publisher (b. 1919)
- o Johnnie Ray, American singer (b. 1927)
- o Sandro Pertini, Italian Socialist politician, former President of the Republic (b. 1896)
- February 27 – Nahum Norbert Glatzer, American scholar (b. 1903)

March

Gary Merrill

- March 4 – Hank Gathers, College Basketball Star (b. 1967)
- March 5 – Gary Merrill, American actor (b. 1915)
- March 6
  - o William Raborn, United States Navy officer, former CIA director (b. 1905)
  - o Joe Sewell, American baseball player (Cleveland Indians) and member of the MLB Hall of Fame (b. 1898)
- March 12 – Philippe Soupault, French poet (b. 1897)
- March 13
  - o Karl Münchinger, German conductor (b. 1915)
  - o Bruno Bettelheim, American child psychologist (b. 1903)
  - o Michael Stewart, British politician, former Foreign Secretary (b. 1906)
- March 14 – Harold Medina, American lawyer, teacher and judge (b. 1888)

- March 17
  - Capucine, French actress and fashion model (b. 1928)
  - Ric Grech, British musician (b. 1946)
- March 18 – Robin Harris, American comedian and actor (b. 1953)
- March 19
  - Andrew Wood, American musician (b. 1966)
  - Oyinkansola Abayomi, Nigerian nationalist and feminist (b. 1897)
  - Neta Lohnes Frazier, American children's author (b. 1890)
- March 20 – Lev Yashin, Russian footballer (b. 1929)
- March 22
  - Bernardo Jaramillo Ossa, Colombian politician (b. 1956)
  - Gerald Bull, Canadian Scientist assassinated by Mossad (b. 1928)
- March 23
  - John Dexter, English theater director (b. 1925)
  - René Enríquez, American actor (b. 1933)
- March 24 – Ray Goulding, American comedian (b. 1922)
- March 26 – Halston, American fashion designer (b. 1932)

April

Greta Garbo

- April 1 – Émile Roche, French economist, radical politician and journalist (b. 1893)
- April 2 – Aldo Fabrizi, Italian actor (b. 1905)
- April 3
  - Sarah Vaughan, American jazz vocalist (b. 1924)
  - Edna Reindel, Surrealist and American Regionalist painter and sculptor (b. 1894)
- April 6 – Alfred Sohn-Rethel, German economist and philosopher (b. 1899)
- April 7 – Ronald Evans, American astronaut, NASA Apollo program (b. 1933)
- April 8
  - Doreen Sloane, British actress (b. 1934)
  - Ryan White, American AIDS activist (b. 1971)
- April 10 – Fortune Gordien, American Olympic athlete (b. 1922)
- April 13 – Luis Trenker, South Tyrolean film producer, director, writer, actor, architect, and alpinist (b. 1892)
- April 14
  - Sabicas, Spanish guitarist (b. 1912)
  - Ahmed Balafrej, Moroccan politician, former Prime Minister and Foreign Minister (b. 1908)
- April 15 – Greta Garbo, Swedish actress (b. 1905)
- April 17 – Ralph Abernathy, American civil rights leader (b. 1926)
- April 18
  - Frédéric Rossif, French film and television director (b. 1922)
  - Gory Guerrero, American wrestler and father of Eddie Guerrero (b. 1921)

- Robert D. Webb, American film director (b. 1903)
- April 19 – Marco Aurelio Robles, Panamanian politician, former President of the Republic (b. 1905)
- April 20 – Horst Sindermann, East German politician, former Prime Minister (b. 1915)
- April 21 – Erté (Romain de Tirtoff), French Art Deco artist (b. 1892)
- April 22 – Albert Salmi, American actor (b. 1928)
- April 23 – Paulette Goddard, American actress (b. 1910)
- April 25 – Dexter Gordon, American jazz saxophonist (b. 1923)
- April 26
  - Myra Bennett, tribute to her tremendous contribution to the people of the Great Northern Peninsula (b. 1890)
  - Carlos Pizarro León-Gómez, Colombian politician (b. 1951)
- April 27 – Bella Spewack, American songwriter (b. 1899)
- April 30 – Joseph E. Johnson, American government official (b. 1895)

May

Walter Bruch behind camera

Sammy Davis, Jr.

Jim Henson

- May 1 – Sunset Carson, American actor (b. 1920)
- May 2
    - William L. Dawson, African-American composer, choir director and professor (b. 1899)
    - David Rappaport, American actor (b. 1951)
- May 3 – Patriarch Pimen I of Moscow, head of the Russian Orthodox Church (b. 1910)
- May 5 – Walter Bruch, German electrical engineer (b. 1908)
- May 6 – Charles Farrell, American actor (b. 1901)
- May 8
    - Tomás Ó Fiaich, Northern Irish cardinal (b. 1923)
    - Luigi Nono, Italian composer (b. 1924)
- May 10
    - Susan Oliver, American actress (b. 1932)

- o Walker Percy, American writer (b. 1916)
- May 12
  - o Andrei Kirilenko, Soviet politician (b. 1906)
  - o Albert Öberg, Swedish athlete (b. 1888)
- May 14 – Franklyn Seales, American actor (b. 1952)
- May 16
  - o Sammy Davis, Jr., American actor, dancer, and singer (b. 1925)
  - o Jim Henson, Muppets creator, American puppeteer and filmmaker (b. 1936)
- May 18 – Jill Ireland, English actress (b. 1936)
- May 21
  - o Max Wall, English actor (b. 1908)
  - o The Hon Mrs Victor Bruce, British record-breaking racing motorist, speedboat racer, aviator (b. 1895)
- May 22
  - o Rocky Graziano, American boxer (b. 1919)
  - o Pat Reid, British soldier and author (b. 1910)
- May 24 – José Del Vecchio, Venezuelan physician and youth baseball promoter (b. 1917)
- May 25
  - o Jeanne de Salzmann, pupil of G. I. Gurdjieff (b. 1889)
  - o Vic Tayback, American actor (b. 1930)
- May 29 – Hussein bin Onn, Malay politician, former Prime Minister (b. 1922)
- May 31 – Willy Spühler, Swiss politician, former President of the Confederation (b. 1902)

June

Rex Harrison

- June 2 – Rex Harrison, English actor (b. 1908)
- June 3 – Robert Noyce, American businessman and inventor (b. 1927)
- June 4
    - Stiv Bators, American singer (The Dead Boys) (b. 1949)
    - Jack Gilford, American actor (b. 1907)
- June 5 – Vasili Kuznetsov, Soviet politician, former provisional head of the State (b. 1901)
- June 6 – Raisa Andriana, Indonesian singer
- June 7
    - Barbara Baxley, American actress (b. 1923)
    - Alfredo Poveda, Ecuadorean military officer and statesman, former head of the State (b. 1926)
- June 8 – José Figueres Ferrer, Costa Rican politician, former President of the Republic (b. 1906)
- June 11 – Vaso Čubrilović, Yugoslav politician, last surviving participant in the conspiracy to kill Archduke Franz Ferdinand of Austria (b. 1897)

- June 12
    - Laura Scales, American educator and college dean (b. 1879)
    - Lord Terence O'Neill, Northern Irish politician, former Prime Minister (b. 1914)
- June 14 – Phillip Henry Bridenbaugh, American football player, coach, and sports figure in the United States (b. 1890)
- June 15 – Leonard Sachs, British actor (b. 1909)
- June 16 – Dame Eva Turner, British soprano (b. 1892)
- June 19 – Steen Eiler Rasmussen, Danish architect and urban planner (b. 1898)
- June 20 – Ina Balin, American actress (b. 1937)
- June 22
    - Ilya Frank, Russian physicist, Nobel Prize laureate (b. 1908)
    - Joseph Murumbi, Kenyan politician, former Vice-President of the Republic (b. 1911)
- June 23 – Harindranath Chattopadhyay, Indian poet, actor and politician, (b. 1898)
- June 24 – Germán Suárez Flamerich, Venezuelan lawyer and politician, former head of State (b. 1907)
- June 29 – Irving Wallace, American writer (b. 1916)
- June 30 – Lynne Carol, British actress (b. 1914)

July

- July 1 – Willem Winkelman, Dutch track and field athlete (b. 1887)
- July 4 – Phil Boggs, American Olympic diver (b. 1949)

- July 6 – Ruth Becker, survivor of the sinking of the RMS Titanic on April 15, 1912 (b. 1899)
- July 7
  - Cazuza, Brazilian poet, singer and composer (b. 1958)
  - Bill Cullen, American game show host (b. 1920)
- July 8 – Howard Duff, American actor (b. 1913)
- July 13 – Lois Moran, American actress (b. 1909)
- July 15
  - Margaret Lockwood, English actress (b. 1916)
  - Enn Roos, Estonian Soviet sculptor (b. 1908)
  - Zaim Topčić, Yugoslav and Bosnian writer (b. 1920)
- July 16 – Isabella Smith Andrews, New Zealand writer (b. 1905)
- July 18
  - Yun Bo-seon, South Korean politician, former President of the Republic (b. 1897)
  - Gerry Boulet, Canadian musician (b. 1946)
  - Yves Chaland, French cartoonist (b. 1957)
  - Karl Menninger, American psychiatrist and a member of the Menninger family (b. 1893)
  - Johnny Wayne, Canadian comedian (b. 1918)
- July 19
  - Egil Aarvik, Norwegian politician, chairman of the Norwegian Nobel Committee (b. 1912)
  - Eddie Quillan, American actor (b. 1907)
- July 21 – Joe Turner, American jazz pianist (b. 1907)
- July 22 – Manuel Puig, Argentinian writer (b. 1932)
- July 23 – Kenjiro Takayanagi, Japanese television engineer (b. 1899)

- July 26 – Brent Mydland, American keyboard player (b. 1952)
- July 27 – René Toribio, Guadeloupean politician (b. 1912)
- July 29 – Bruno Kreisky, Austrian Social Democratic politician, former Federal Chancellor (b. 1911)
- July 30 – Ian Gow, British politician (b. 1937)
- July 31 – Fernando Sancho, Spanish actor (b. 1916)

August

Pearl Bailey

- August 1
  - Norbert Elias, German sociologist of Jewish descent (b. 1897)
  - Willard L. Beaulac, a United States Diplomat (b. 1899)
  - Robert Krieps, Luxembourgian Social Democratic politician (b. 1922)
- August 2 – Edwin Richfield, British actor (b. 1921)
- August 4
  - Mathias Goeritz, Mexican-German artist (b. 1915)
  - Ettore Maserati, Italian automotive engineer (b. 1894)
- August 6

- o Lemuel C. Shepherd, Jr., four-star general of the United States Marine Corps (b. 1896)
  - o Jacques Soustelle, French politician and anthropologist (b. 1912)
- August 9
  - o Dorothy Appleby, American film actress (b. 1906)
  - o Joe Mercer, English footballer (b. 1914)
- August 12 – Dorothy Mackaill, British-born American actress (b. 1903)
- August 15 – Viktor Tsoi, Russian singer, actor and poet (b. 1962)
- August 17 – Pearl Bailey, American singer and actress (b. 1918)
- August 18 – B. F. Skinner, American psychologist (b. 1904)
- August 22
  - o Luigi Dadaglio, Italian Catholic Cardinal (b. 1914)
  - o Patrick McAlinney, Irish actor (b. 1913)
- August 23 – David Rose, British-born American songwriter, composer, arranger and orchestra leader (b. 1910)
- August 24 – Sergei Dovlatov, Russian short-story writer and novelist (b. 1941)
- August 26 – Mário Pinto de Andrade, Angolan politician and poet (b. 1928)
- August 27
  - o Raymond St. Jacques, American actor (b. 1930)
  - o Stevie Ray Vaughan, American guitarist (b. 1954)
- August 31 – Sergey Nikolayevich Volkov, Russian figure skater (b. 1949)

September

Samuel Doe

Xu Xiangqian

- September 1 – Geir Hallgrímsson, Icelandic politician, former Prime Minister (b. 1925)
- September 2 – John Bowlby, British psychologist and psychiatrist (b. 1907)
- September 4 – Irene Dunne, American actress (b. 1898)
- September 6 – Tom Fogerty, American musician (b. 1941)
- September 7
  - A. J. P. Taylor, English historian (b. 1906)
  - Ahti Karjalainen, Finnish politician, former Prime Minister (b. 1923)

- September 9
    - Samuel Doe, Liberian military officer and statesman, head of state from 1980 (b. 1951)
    - Nicola Abbagnano, Italian philosopher (b. 1901)
- September 16 – Len Hutton, English cricketer (b. 1916)
- September 17 – Lilí Martínez, Cuban pianist and arranger (b. 1917)
- September 19
    - Hermes Pan, American choreographer (b. 1910)
    - Walter Tucker, Canadian politician (b. 1899)
- September 21 – Xu Xiangqian, Communist military leader in the People's Republic of China, former Defense minister (b. 1901)
- September 25 – Togyu Okumura, Japanese modern painter (b. 1889)
    - Prafulla Chandra Sen, Indian politician and Chief Minister of West Bengal (b. 1897)
- September 26 – Alberto Moravia, Italian novelist (b. 1907)
- September 30 – Patrick White, Australian writer, Nobel Prize laureate (b. 1912)

October

Beatrice Hutton

Leonard Bernstein

- October 1 – Curtis LeMay, United States Air Force general (b. 1906)
- October 3
    - Stefano Casiraghi, Italian husband of Princess Caroline of Monaco (b. 1960)
    - André Grabar, historian of Romanesque art and the art of the Eastern Roman Empire (b. 1896)
- October 4
    - Jill Bennett, British actress (b. 1931)
    - Avis Bunnage, British actress (b. 1923)
- October 5 – Peter Taylor, English footballer and manager (b. 1928)
- October 7
    - Beatrice Hutton, Australian architect (b. 1893)
    - Rashid bin Said Al-Maktoum, Vice-President and Prime Minister of United Arab Emirates and Emir (Ruler) of Dubai (b. 1912)
    - Juan José Arévalo, Guatemalan politician, former President of the Republic (b. 1904)
    - Grim Natwick, American animator (b. 1890)

- October 8 – William H. Harrison (Wyoming Congressman), American politician who served as a Republican U.S. Representative (b. 1896)
- October 12 – Rifaat el-Mahgoub, Speaker of the Egyptian Assembly (b. 1926)
- October 13
  - Douglas Edwards, American television news anchor (b. 1917)
  - Lê Đức Thọ, Vietnamese general and politician, recipient of the Nobel Peace Prize (b. 1911)
- October 14 – Leonard Bernstein, American composer and conductor (b. 1918)
- October 15
  - Delphine Seyrig, French actress (b. 1932)
  - Helen Bray, American actress (b. 1889)
- October 16 – Art Blakey, American jazz musician (b. 1919)
- October 20 – Joel McCrea, American actor (b. 1905)
- October 21 – Dany Chamoun, Lebanese politician (b. 1934)
- October 22 – Louis Althusser, French philosopher (b. 1918)
- October 23 – Zephania Mothopeng, South African politician, leader of the Pan-Africanist Congress (PAC) (b. 1913)
- October 26 – William S. Paley, American radio and television executive (b. 1901)
- October 27
  - Xavier Cugat, American band leader (b. 1900)
  - Jacques Demy, French film director (b. 1931)
  - Helmut Maandi, Estonian statesman (b. 1906)
  - Elliott Roosevelt, American writer, son of President Franklin D. Roosevelt (b. 1910)
  - Ugo Tognazzi, Italian actor (b. 1922)

- October 29 – William F. Smith, American lawyer and former Attorney General of the United States (b. 1917)

November

Mary Martin

Robert Hofstadter

Roald Dahl

- November 3 – Mary Martin, American actress (b. 1913)

- November 4 – Henry Cravatte, Luxembourgian Social Democratic politician, former Deputy Prime Minister (b. 1911)
- November 5 – Meir Kahane, American rabbi and political figure (b. 1932)
- November 7 – Lawrence Durrell, British writer (b. 1912)
- November 11
  - Yiannis Ritsos, Greek poet (b. 1909)
  - Sadi Irmak, Turkish politician, former Prime Minister (b. 1904)
  - Rusty Goodman, American gospel singer of the Happy Goodman Family (b. 1931)
- November 12 – Eve Arden, American actress (b. 1908)
- November 13 – Don Chaffey, British film director (b. 1917)
- November 17 – Robert Hofstadter, American physicist, Nobel Prize laureate (b. 1915)
- November 20 – Herbert Kegel, German conductor (b. 1920)
- November 23
  - Roald Dahl, Welsh writer (b. 1916)
  - Nguyễn Văn Tâm, South Vietnamese politician, former Prime Minister (b. 1893)
- November 24
  - Helga Feddersen, German actress (b. 1930)
  - Dodie Smith, English novelist and playwright (b. 1896)
- November 26 – Feng Youlan, Chinese philosopher (b. 1895)
- November 27
  - David White, American actor (b. 1916)
  - Frank Edward Figgures, British civil servant, first secretary-general of the European Free Trade Association (b. 1910)

December

Robert Cummings

Tunku Abdul Rahman

Joan Bennett

Friedrich Dürrenmatt

- December 1 – Sergio Corbucci, Italian film director (b. 1927)
- December 2
  - Aaron Copland, American composer (b. 1900)
  - Robert Cummings, American actor (b. 1908)
- December 4 – Naoto Tajima, Japanese athlete (b. 1912)
- December 6
  - Pavlos Sidiropoulos, Greek singer and songwriter (b. 1948)
  - Tunku Abdul Rahman, Malaysian politician, former Prime Minister (b. 1903)
- December 7
  - Reinaldo Arenas, Cuban writer (b. 1943)
  - Dee Clark, American soul singer (b. 1938)
  - Joan Bennett, American actress (b. 1910)
- December 8
  - Boris Kochno, Russian poet, dancer, and librettist (b. 1906)
  - Tadeusz Kantor, Polish painter, assemblage designer and theatre director (b. 1915)
  - Enrico Coveri, Italian fashion designer and entrepreneur (b. 1952)
  - Martin Ritt, American film director (b. 1914)
- December 9 – Mike Mazurki, American actor and wrestler (b. 1909)
- December 10 – Armand Hammer, American business tycoon (b. 1898)
- December 11 – Concha Piquer, Spanish singer and actress (b. 1908)
- December 13 – Alice Marble, American tennis champion (b. 1913)

- December 14
    - Friedrich Dürrenmatt, Swiss writer (b. 1921)
    - Francisco Gabilondo Soler, Mexican singer (b. 1907)
    - Edmund Franklin Ward, illustrated for the *Saturday Evening Post* (b. 1892)
- December 15 – Ed Parker, American Kenpo founder (b. 1931)
- December 16
    - Douglas Campbell, American World War I pilot (b. 1896)
    - Jackie Mittoo, Jamaican musician (b. 1948)
- December 18 – Anne Revere, American actress (b. 1903)
- December 20 – Elmo Tanner, American singer and whistler (b. 1910)
- December 24
    - Tammy Homolka, Canadian murder victim (b. 1975)
    - Thorbjørn Egner, Norwegian author (b. 1912)
- December 28 – Kiel Martin, American actor (b. 1944)
- December 31
    - Vasily Lazarev, Soviet cosmonaut (b. 1928)
    - George Allen, American football coach (Washington Redskins) and member of the Pro Football Hall of Fame (b. 1918)
    - Elsie Allen, a Native American Pomo basket weaver (b. 1899)

Nobel Prizes

- Physics – Jerome Isaac Friedman, Henry Way Kendall, and Richard Edward Taylor
- Chemistry – Elias James Corey
- Physiology or Medicine – Joseph Murray, E. Donnall Thomas
- Literature – Octavio Paz
- Peace – Mikhail Gorbachev
- Bank of Sweden Prize in Economic Sciences in Memory of Alfred Nobel – Harry Markowitz, Merton Miller, William F. Sharpe

In the News.

Saddam Hussein orders Iraq invasion of Neighboring Kuwait.

Operation Desert Shield Begins as the United States and UK send troops to Kuwait.

Americas Favorite animated family "The Simpsons " is aired on Fox for the first time.

The demolition of the Berlin Wall officially begins during June.

Poll Tax introduced in UK causing mass demonstrations who claimed the tax moved the tax burden from the rich to the poor.

Margaret Thatcher announces her resignation as British PM after John Major is chosen to lead the country and conservative party.

The Leaning Tower of Pisa is closed to the public due to safety concerns of it falling over.

Nelson Mandella released from prison and becomes leader of the African National Congress (ANC)

Tim Berners-Lee publishes a more formal proposal for the World Wide Web and the first web page is written.

Channel Tunnel workers from the United Kingdom and France meet 40 meters beneath the English Channel seabed, establishing the first ground connection between the United Kingdom and the mainland of Europe since the last ice age.

West Germany Wins 1990 World Cup in Italy.

Depletion of the Ozone Layer is discovered above the North Pole.

Popular Films - Home Alone, Ghost, Dances with Wolves, Pretty Woman, Teenage Mutant Ninja Turtles, The Hunt for Red October, Total Recall, Die Hard 2, Dick Tracy, Edward Scissorhands,The Godfather Part III.

1990 Calender.

January 1990
Sun	Mon	Tue	Wed	Thu	Fri	Sat
	1	2	3	4	5	6
7	8	9	10	11	12	13
14	15	16	17	18	19	20
21	22	23	24	25	26	27
28	29	30	31			

February 1990
Sun	Mon	Tue	Wed	Thu	Fri	Sat
				1	2	3
4	5	6	7	8	9	10
11	12	13	14	15	16	17
18	19	20	21	22	23	24
25	26	27	28			

March 1990
Sun	Mon	Tue	Wed	Thu	Fri	Sat
				1	2	3
4	5	6	7	8	9	10
11	12	13	14	15	16	17
18	19	20	21	22	23	24
25	26	27	28	29	30	31

April 1990
Sun	Mon	Tue	Wed	Thu	Fri	Sat
1	2	3	4	5	6	7
8	9	10	11	12	13	14
15	16	17	18	19	20	21
22	23	24	25	26	27	28
29	30					

May 1990
Sun	Mon	Tue	Wed	Thu	Fri	Sat
		1	2	3	4	5
6	7	8	9	10	11	12
13	14	15	16	17	18	19
20	21	22	23	24	25	26
27	28	29	30	31		

June 1990
Sun	Mon	Tue	Wed	Thu	Fri	Sat
					1	2
3	4	5	6	7	8	9
10	11	12	13	14	15	16
17	18	19	20	21	22	23
24	25	26	27	28	29	30

July 1990
Sun	Mon	Tue	Wed	Thu	Fri	Sat
1	2	3	4	5	6	7
8	9	10	11	12	13	14
15	16	17	18	19	20	21
22	23	24	25	26	27	28
29	30	31				

August 1990
Sun	Mon	Tue	Wed	Thu	Fri	Sat
			1	2	3	4
5	6	7	8	9	10	11
12	13	14	15	16	17	18
19	20	21	22	23	24	25
26	27	28	29	30	31	

September 1990
Sun	Mon	Tue	Wed	Thu	Fri	Sat
						1
2	3	4	5	6	7	8
9	10	11	12	13	14	15
16	17	18	19	20	21	22
23	24	25	26	27	28	29
30						

October 1990
Sun	Mon	Tue	Wed	Thu	Fri	Sat
	1	2	3	4	5	6
7	8	9	10	11	12	13
14	15	16	17	18	19	20
21	22	23	24	25	26	27
28	29	30	31			

November 1990
Sun	Mon	Tue	Wed	Thu	Fri	Sat
				1	2	3
4	5	6	7	8	9	10
11	12	13	14	15	16	17
18	19	20	21	22	23	24
25	26	27	28	29	30	

December 1990
Sun	Mon	Tue	Wed	Thu	Fri	Sat
						1
2	3	4	5	6	7	8
9	10	11	12	13	14	15
16	17	18	19	20	21	22
23	24	25	26	27	28	29
30	31